Her eyes widened as she opened the lid. She was astounded to see a spectacular Russian lacquer box in the shape of a violin. Underneath the glossy lacquer surface of the violin box was a marvellously designed pattern of a sunflower.

Mayuri was mesmerised by the glossy finish of the violin-shaped lacquer box which had been placed so perfectly inside the lapis lazuli box. Mayuri held the lacquer box tightly in her hands as the plane took off from Moscow. Mayuri's emotions and thoughts took a trip down memory lane. The Russian lacquer box was serendipitously similar to the Japanese lacquer box she had left in her room back in Kobe. Mayuri was filled with awe at this amazingly magical connection and instantly thought that this was **Ichi Go Ichi E** (one time meeting is like a lifetime of meaning and opportunity).

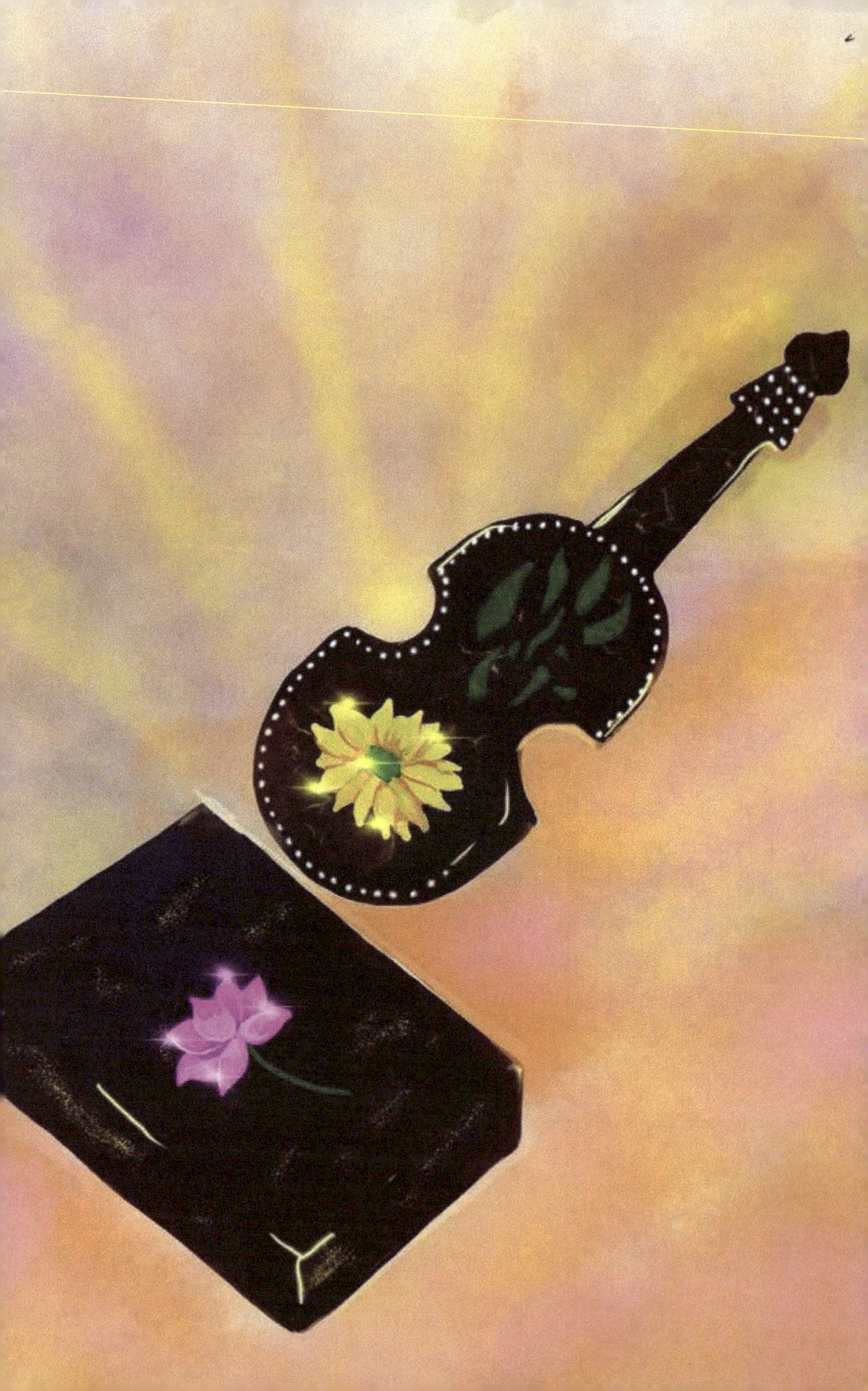

The Lacquer Box

Parul Rajpopat Thakker
Illustrations by Radhika Iyer

Bumblebee Books
London

BUMBLEBEE PAPERBACK EDITION

Illustrations by Radhika Iyer

A CIP catalogue record for this title is available from the British Library.

ISBN: 978-1-83934-639-2

Bumblebee Books is an imprint of Olympia Publishers.

First Published in 2022

Bumblebee Books
Tallis House
2 Tallis Street
London
EC4Y 0AB

Printed in Great Britain

www.olympiapublishers.com

Dedication

With all that we are facing in today's world (natural disasters, wars, the pandemic, etc), this book is dedicated to all the children of the world for their safe and happy future. May they always have peace in their environment and be inspired to live a meaningful life.

Royalties received from this book will be gifted to various children's organizations.

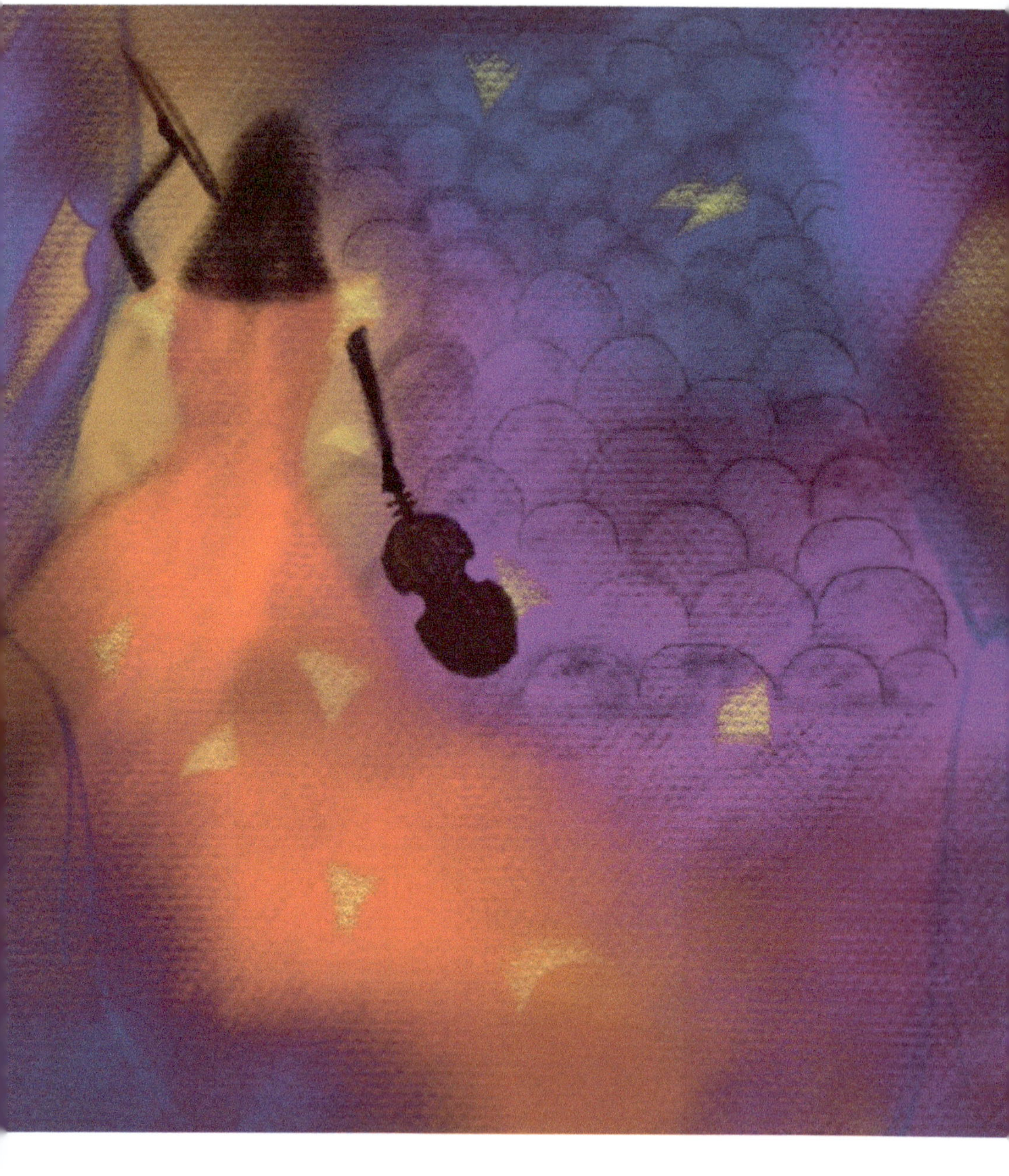

The thunderous applause echoed inside the Bolshoi Ballet Theatre. Matsumoto Mayuri could feel her heart pounding as she bowed to acknowledge the standing ovation. She was overwhelmed with the grand response she received from the audience after her violin performance of Tchaikovsky's 'Swan Lake'.

Soon after the concert, she received a gift from the members of the orchestra for her brilliant performance. It was a small and gorgeous stoneware container made of mystical, deep blue, precious-looking stone. The Russian musicians handed this ineffable stone box to her explaining the significance of the lapis lazuli treasure chest from Afghanistan.

There was something very profound and beautiful about this mysterious, galactic, dark blue stone with white marble streaks – it symbolised our blue planet in the dark blue universe. The musicians further explained that enclosed within the lapis lazuli box is yet another treasure which we all want to always honour and protect. They told her to open this special lapis lazuli box after she takes off for her flight back home to Japan. Mayuri was excited and deeply touched by their gesture. She graciously accepted their warm gift, thanking them for their kind hospitality during her stay in Moscow.

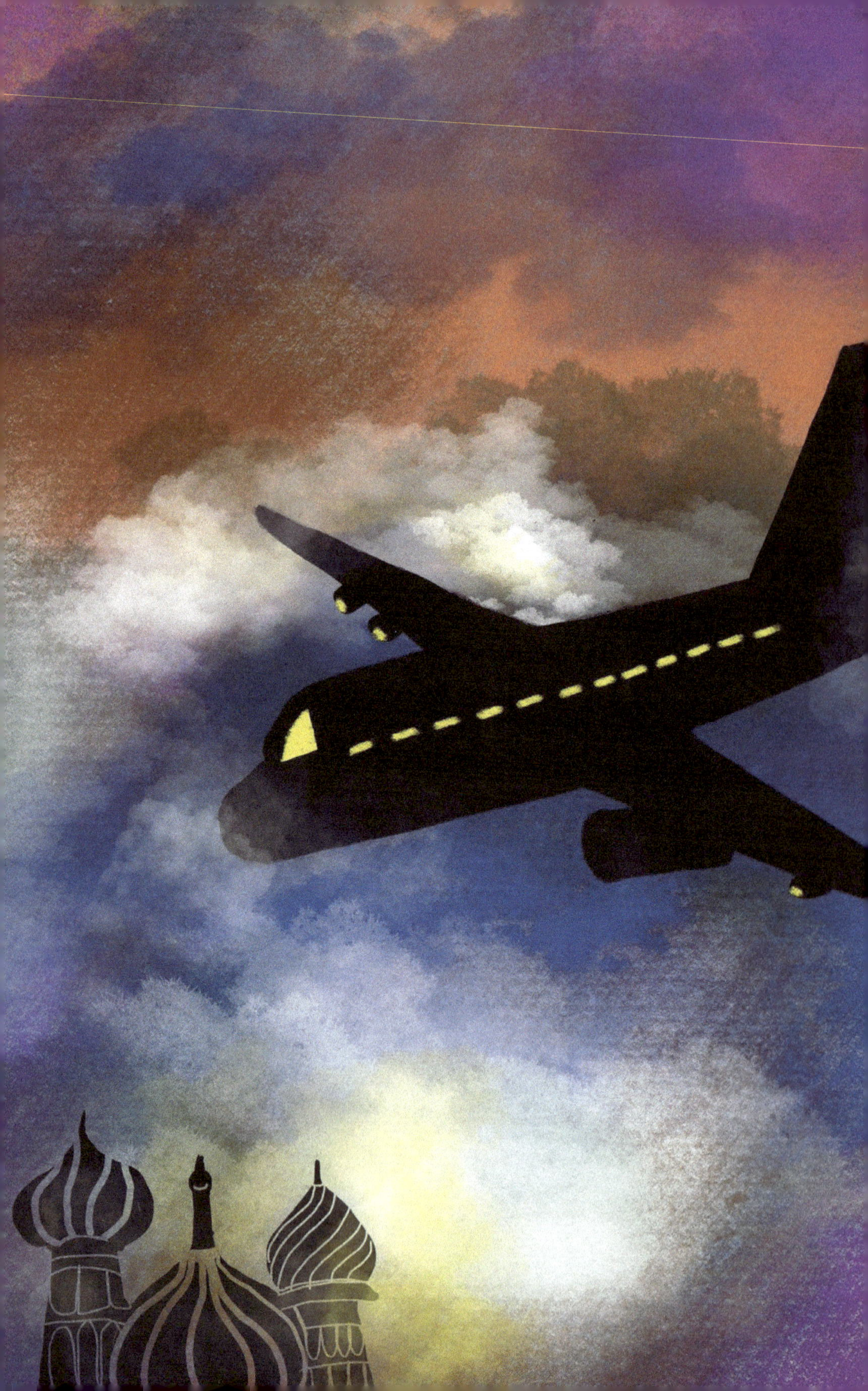

That same night Mayuri boarded her flight back to Osaka. Soon after she was comfortably seated by the window with her seat belt fastened, Mayuri started reminiscing about her unforgettable experience in Russia. She kept recollecting about her remarkable performance with the Moscow Orchestra and couldn't wait to open the lapis lazuli box. She delved into her bag and carefully took out the heavy, exquisite blue stone box.

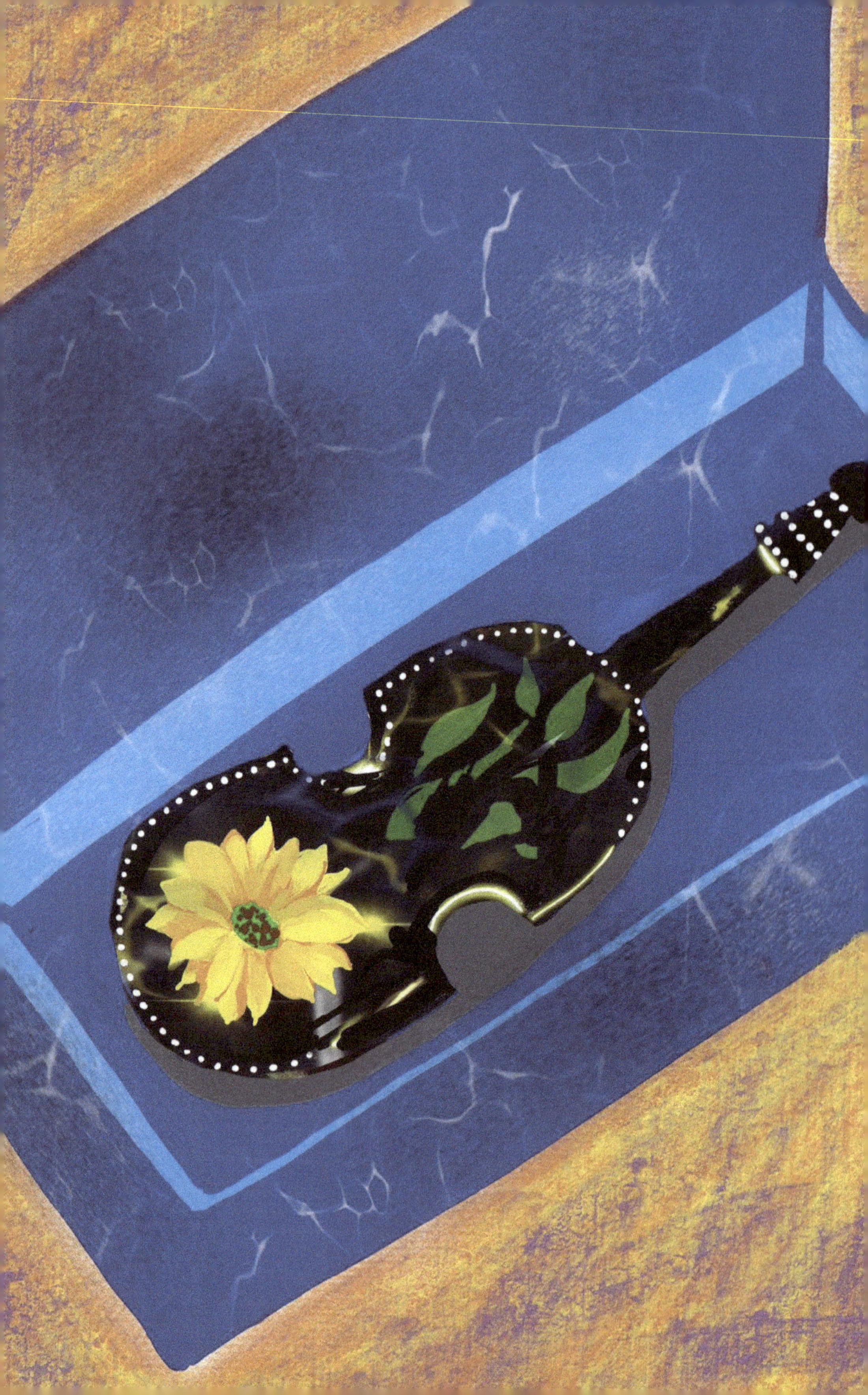

The Japanese lacquer box which she held so close to her heart back home was her mother's most cherished possession. **En** (destiny) had played its part for Mayuri to have received this Russian lacquer box, which she was now holding physically close to her heart. It was so similar in texture and sheen to her mother's box. Staring admirably at the violin shaped Russian lacquer box, Mayuri experienced an epiphany. The wooden violin lacquer box was incredibly well-protected by being enclosed in the blue earth-like lapis lazuli box. As the flight ascended higher into the dark blue sky, Mayuri was transported back to her childhood days twenty-five years ago.

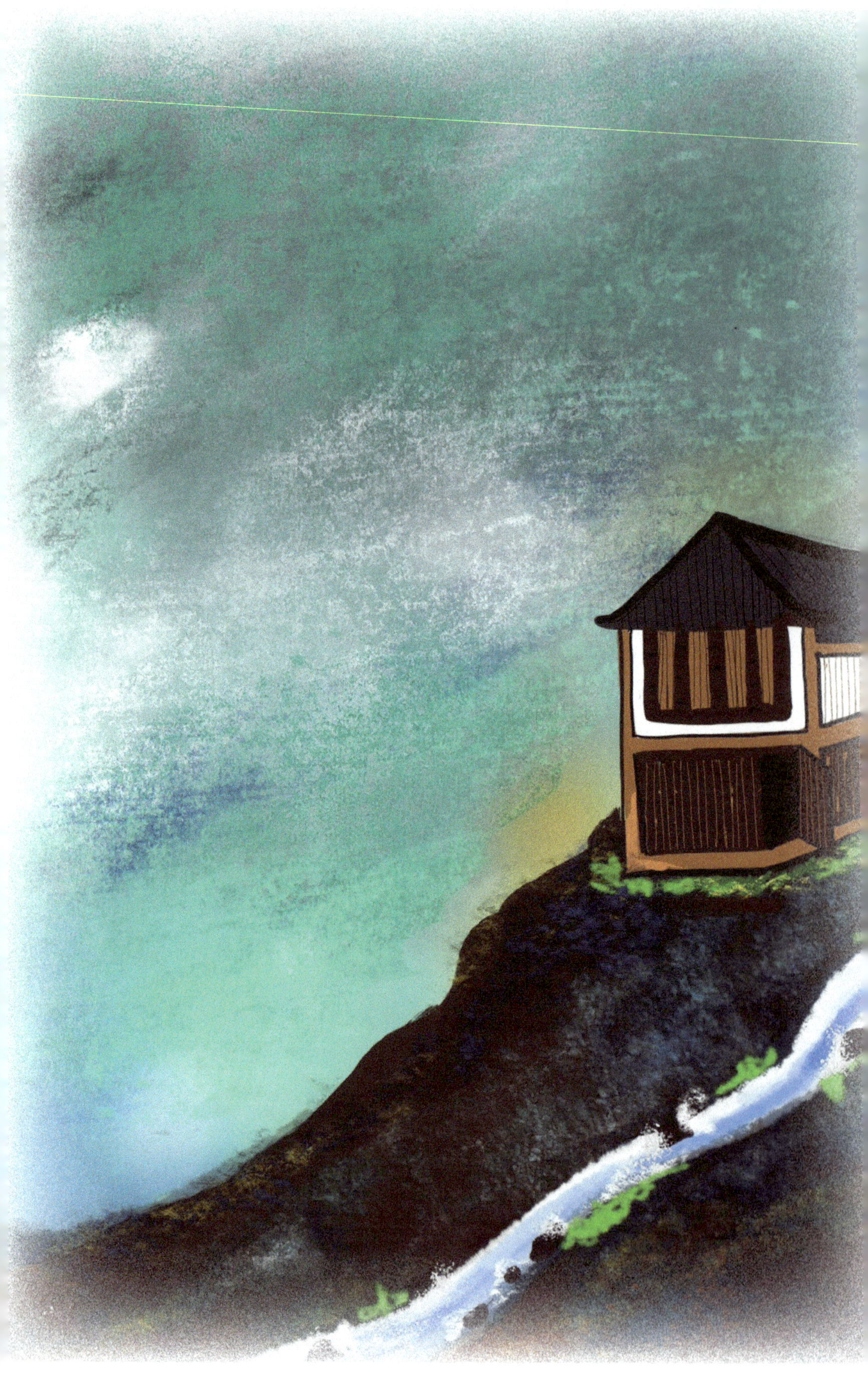

Kadota Sensei lived in a small house on Rokko Hill. She was a strict disciplinarian violin teacher. Sensei often made ten-year-old Mayuri cry when she reprimanded her on her dispassionate performance of the vibrato. On one such day, Mayuri could no longer bear the authority of Kadota Sensei. Frustrated and upset, Mayuri darted out of her Sensei's home and made up her mind that she was done with violin lessons forever!

Tears gushed down Mayuri's cheeks as she ran down the hill towards her home. She slid open the door, threw her shoes off and without even saying **Tadaima** (Japanese greeting upon entering one's own home), Mayuri stomped up the creaky wooden stairs with her violin case. On entering her mother's room, she saw her mother gazing intently at an object in her hand. A closer look revealed a beautiful shiny black box that her mother was looking at with great fondness and admiration.

Mayuri realised that this box was very precious to her mother. She watched with great intrigue as her mother lovingly wiped the glossy rectangular shaped box with a soft beige chamois. This was not the first time that Mayuri had seen her mother take such loving care of this box.

"**Okaasan** (mother), why do you love this box so much?" asked Mayuri as she stepped into her mother's room. It was a question that had long prevailed in her mind.

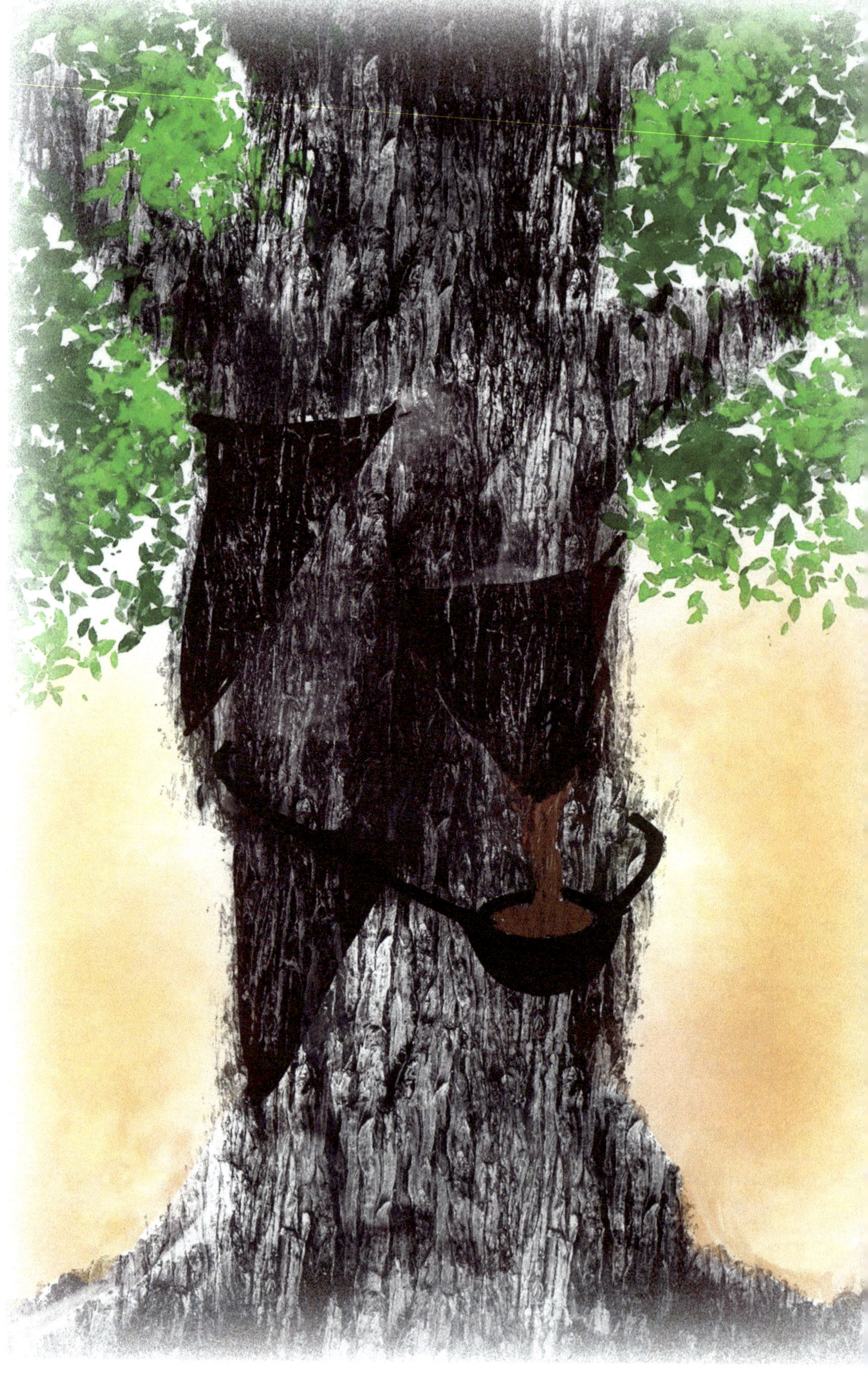

Mayuri's mother smiled compassionately and while gently stroking Mayuri's head, she told her it was a special gift from her father who passed away when Mayuri was just a toddler. She began to explain how her **Otousan** (father) used to go to the woods to collect resin from the lacquer tree to create beautiful works of art. She explained the intricacies involved in the process of creating this beautifully glowing black lacquer box. The strenuous application of layer upon layer of the lacquer polish is what gave this perfect glow.

She told Mayuri how her father spent hours in the forest making deliberate cuts on the trunk of the lacquer tree to make it secrete a mysterious kind of healing sap.

Okaasan spoke of the process as being painful because it affected the skin of all those arborists, like her father, who needed to collect the sap as soon as the trunk started secreting it. The same lacquer tree sap, or resin, which is used as polish on wooden objects to attain its utmost beauty, also has a magical ability to heal its own bark! The wonders of nature never cease to awe us. Mayuri's mother further drew her attention to the intricate **Kirikane** (traditional Japanese inlay work) of the magnificent pink lotus flower on the lid of the pristine box.

The sadness in her eyes accompanied with her melancholic expression seemed to remind Mayuri's mother of the struggles she had faced in her own life. The lacquer box was bequeathed from **Otousan** as something symbolic of everything they went through in their lives together.

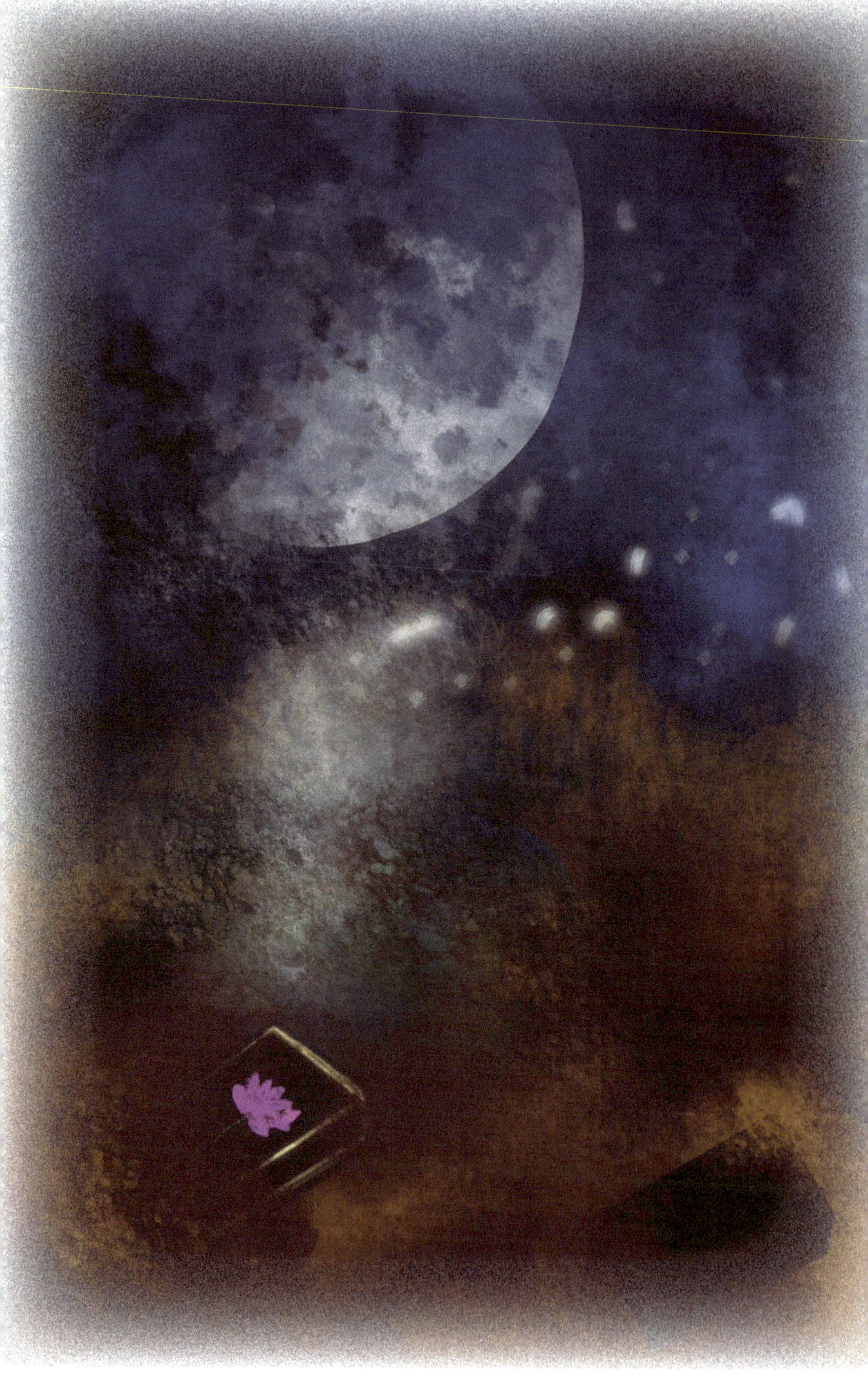

Early next morning, way before sunrise in the Land of the Rising Sun, the earth rumbled, roared and shook violently. The devastation all around was beyond imagination. The Matsumotos' home was destroyed like many other homes in the neighbourhood. Their house had become a heap of rubble between the earth and sky!

Buried under the debris that was once her home, Mayuri cried out for help. Upon hearing her cries a neighbour pulled her out and Mayuri looked around in the darkness, shivering in the cold and creepy surrounding. Panic began to engulf her when she shouted out to her mother and heard no response. An eerie silence travelled through her entire being as she realized a distressed feeling of deep loss.

But nothing stopped Mayuri from rummaging through the debris, throwing aside planks of wood and rubble desperately looking for her mother. Amidst the shambles something shiny caught her attention. She cleared her way to the sparkling object and found that it was the lid of her mother's precious lacquer box. Though covered with a layer of dust, it still managed to glisten. A short distance away lay the rest of the box, upside down and damaged.

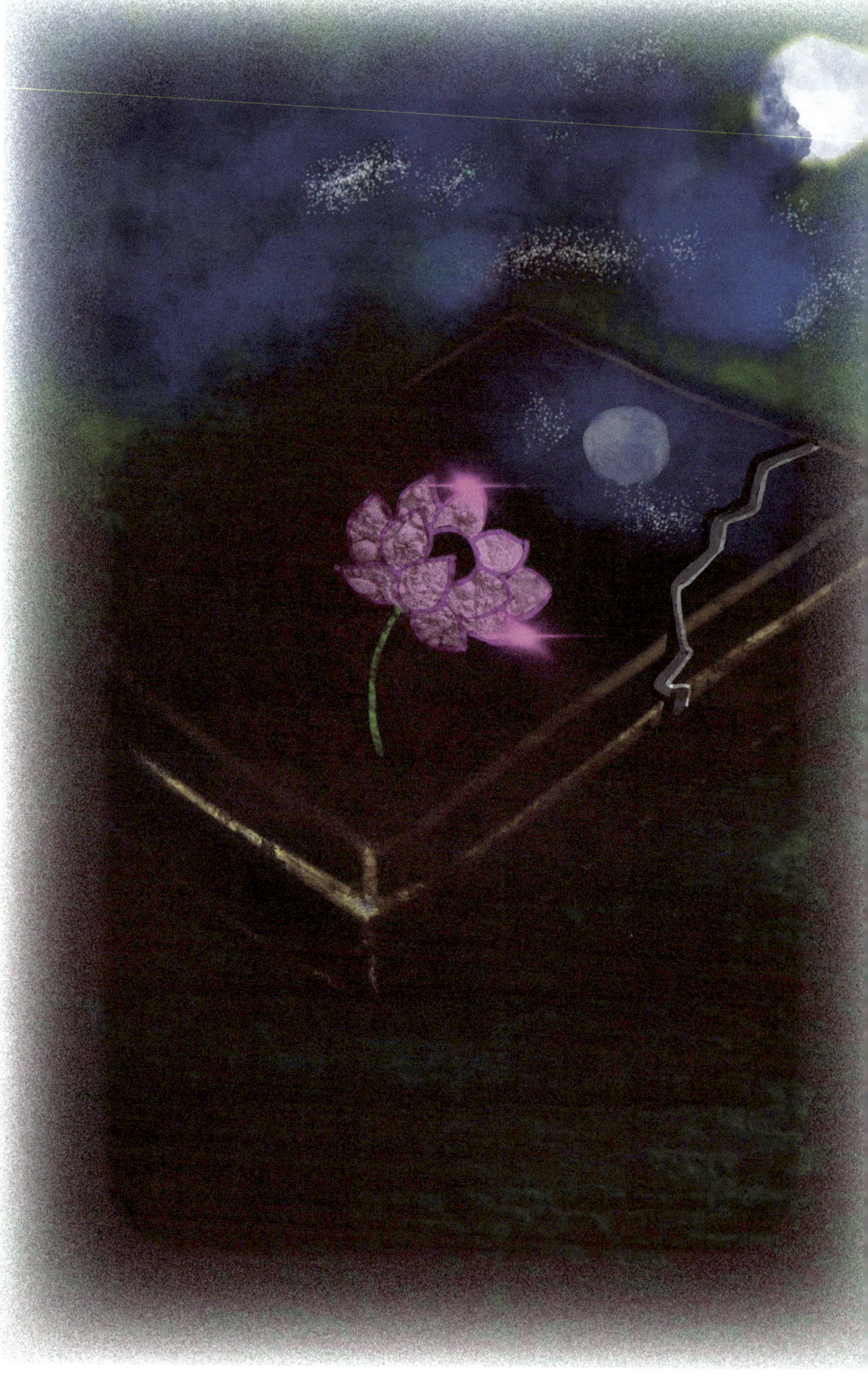

As Mayuri picked up the lid and wiped it with her bare hands she noticed that it had a deep crack. The beautiful lotus pattern had miraculously remained intact. She picked up the box, put on the lid and held it close to her heart. Teardrops continued to fall silently on top of the box.

The tears gradually cleared off the dust on the box. Mayuri used her pyjama sleeve to wipe off the remaining dust which made the surface of the lacquer box clear and shiny once again. It was just like she had seen it in her mother's hands the night before. And it was as though the universe had sent a message to her mother the night before to prepare Mayuri for what was to come.

The moon lit up the darkened sky as Mayuri held the box with angst. However, the reflection of the moon and stars on the shiny lacquer box captivated her. As she struggled her way out of the rubble, she felt she had captured the moon and stars in her hands along with the pristine pink lotus! Holding tightly on to her mother's cherished possession, Mayuri felt she can quietly rest outside the rubble of her home.

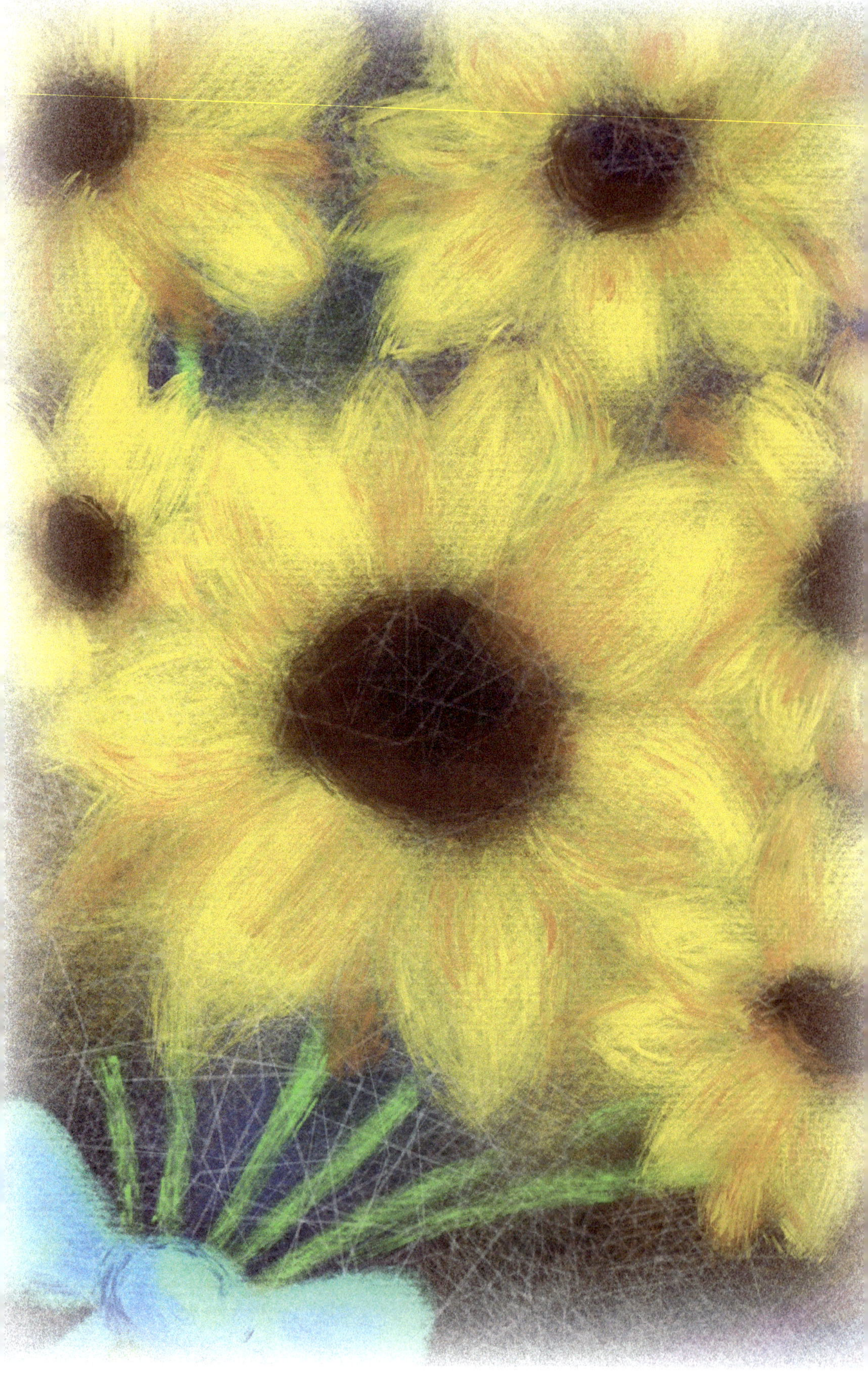

Upon waking up, Mayuri found herself lying in a hospital bed with her head and pinkie finger bandaged up. She had no recollection of how she got there. But she felt at ease the moment she heard the familiar sound of the Zen temple dongs. The resonating sound gave her a sense of comfort. Mayuri now knew she was somewhere near her home because it was with this daily 6am temple dongs that her mother came to wake her up for school every day.

Listening to the soothing sound of the **Kane no Ne** (sound of the ringing bells), Mayuri was hoping and praying that her mother would come to wake her up.

But her mother never came.

On the side table of her hospital bed lay the now even more precious lacquer box. Mayuri picked it up slowly and carefully looked at the deep crack on its lid. While scrutinizing the depth of the crack, she began to understand the depth of her mother's words. She observed the multiple layers of lacquer polish through the crack and how these deep layers had finally created the perfectly finished lacquer box. It dawned on her that there was so much pain, hardship, love and compassion which went into the making of this box. Mayuri lay in bed comforted by the thought of having salvaged this box.

A few days later Kadota Sensei visited Mayuri at the hospital. She brought Mayuri a bright bouquet of sunflowers which felt like sunshine had entered the room!

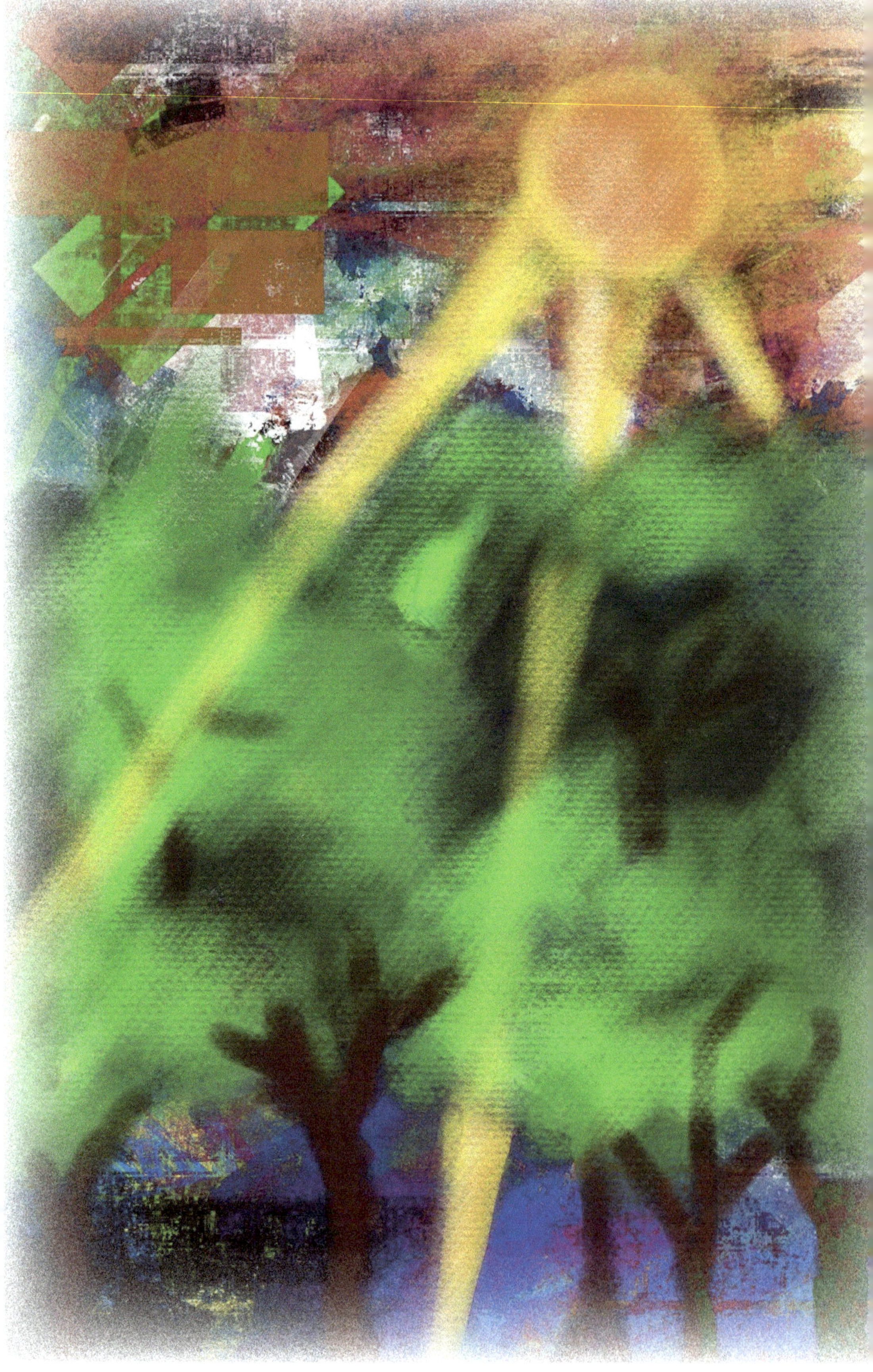

Sensei told Mayuri that she would now be living with her. They walked out of the hospital together. Mayuri's left hand held on to Sensei's hand and her right hand tightly held the lacquer box. Walking slowly, they stopped in front of what was once the Matsumoto home. Mayuri stood there silently lost in her own thoughts and memories. Then suddenly she took the bouquet of bright yellow and orange sunflowers from Sensei and laid it on top of the remains of what she once knew as home.

Time does not stand still. It passed by quickly like the gushing river outside Sensei's home splashing on littles rocks that came along its way. Mayuri felt her life had to stream along in a similar manner overcoming obstacles along the way.

One day Sensei decided to take Mayuri up to the mountains for a change of atmosphere. Walking up to the mountain, they passed through forests that came alive with the sounds of birds and animals. Sensei and Mayuri held hands as they enjoyed the beauty of all the flora in various shades of green. The air was crisp and fresh. Every now and then they would stop to admire the **Komorebi** (sunbeams filtering through the shaded branches of trees) which bathed the forest with a welcoming warmth. Ever so often, as they continued their walk, Sensei would stop for **Shinrinyoku** (forest bathing) to allow Mayuri's heart and mind to heal. The environment of the forest allowed Mayuri to absorb nature's healing energy through all her five senses.

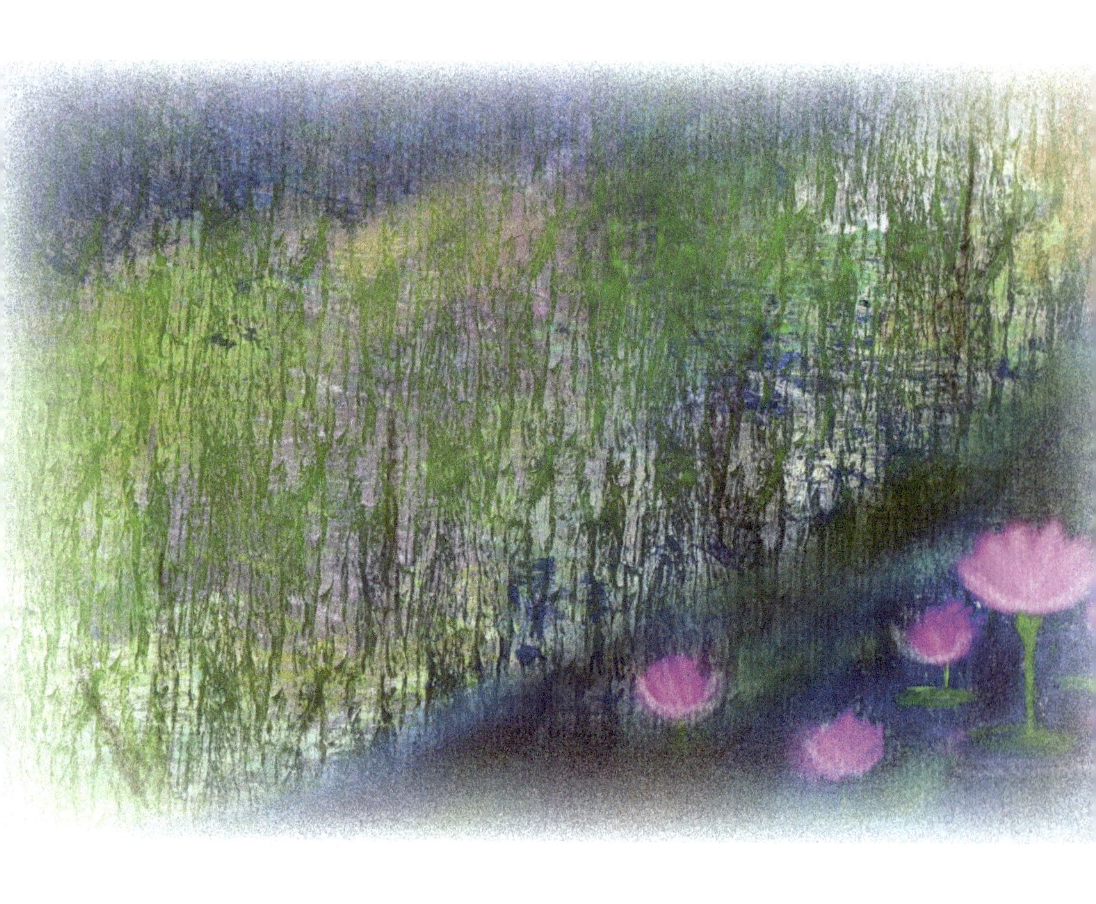

They continued their walk up the mountain and stopped on reaching a serene and tranquil pond. Mayuri could not help but notice how murky the water was! What further caught her attention was a perfect pink lotus emerging from the muddy water. The image of the pink lotus on her mother's lacquer box flashed before her eyes! A sense of pure joy enveloped her as she realized that there is something beautiful evolving from the dark and docile.

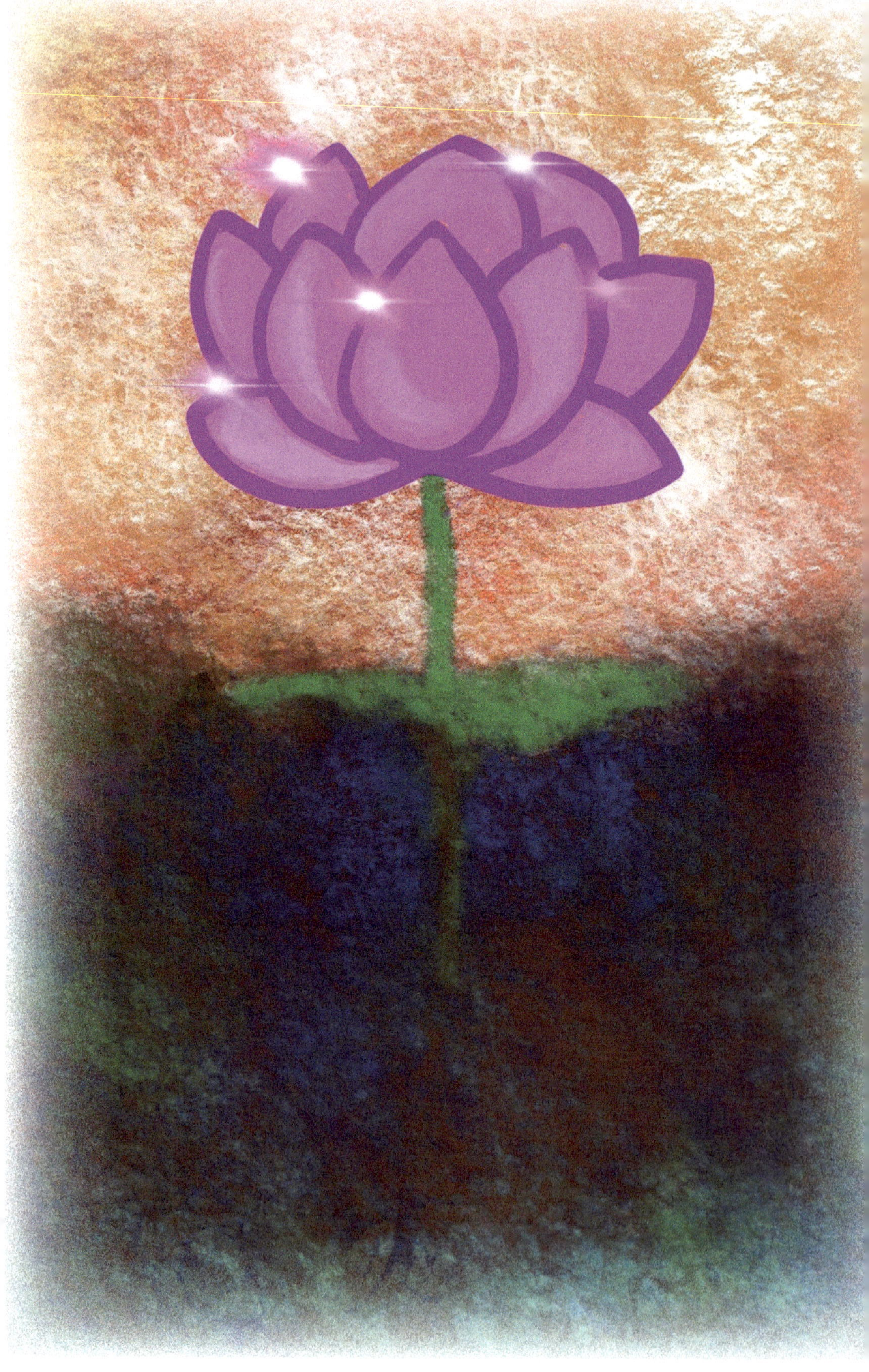

The lotus flower in all its glory stood out above and beyond its surrounding darkness. Mayuri asked Sensei to pluck the lotus for her. Sensei hesitated at first but then gladly bent over and plucked the lotus out of the pond for Mayuri. It had occurred to Sensei that **Hana o Rou Sureba, Kaori Koromo ni Mitsu** (hold on to a flower and its fragrance will cling on to your clothes and influence your emotions). Even though the lotus has no fragrance, Sensei was certain that its impact will bring a change in Mayuri.

All the way home Mayuri admired the lotus and felt rejuvenated and enlightened. Upon reaching home, Mayuri ran up to her room to fetch the lacquer box.

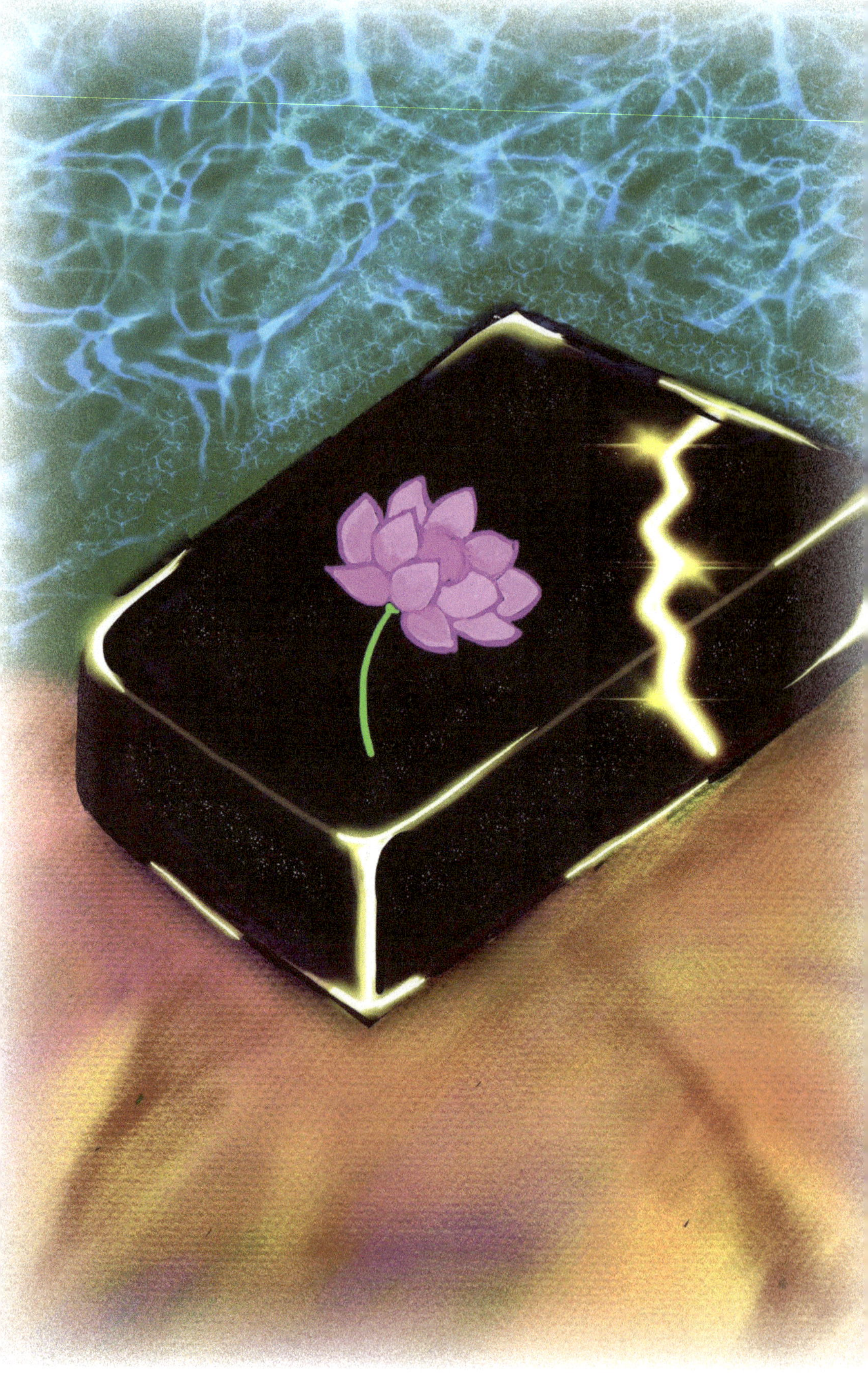

She was pleasantly surprised to find that the crack on the lid had been repaired. Sensei had secretly taken the box for **Kintsugi** (filling in of the crack with gold). Mayuri was filled with inexplainable joy on seeing the gold filling in the crack which simply added more beauty to the box. It added glamour and at the same time portrayed the **Wabi Sabi** effect (an aesthetic Japanese philosophy that within any imperfection there is the beauty of perfection). The new look touched Mayuri's mind and soul beyond her own understanding. Tears welled up in her eyes. Sensei was silently watching Mayuri from the bedroom doorway and gently wiped her own tears as she walked away. Sensei then returned to Mayuri's room holding a slightly bigger brand-new violin for Mayuri. Her old one was lost amongst all her other belongings in the earthquake.

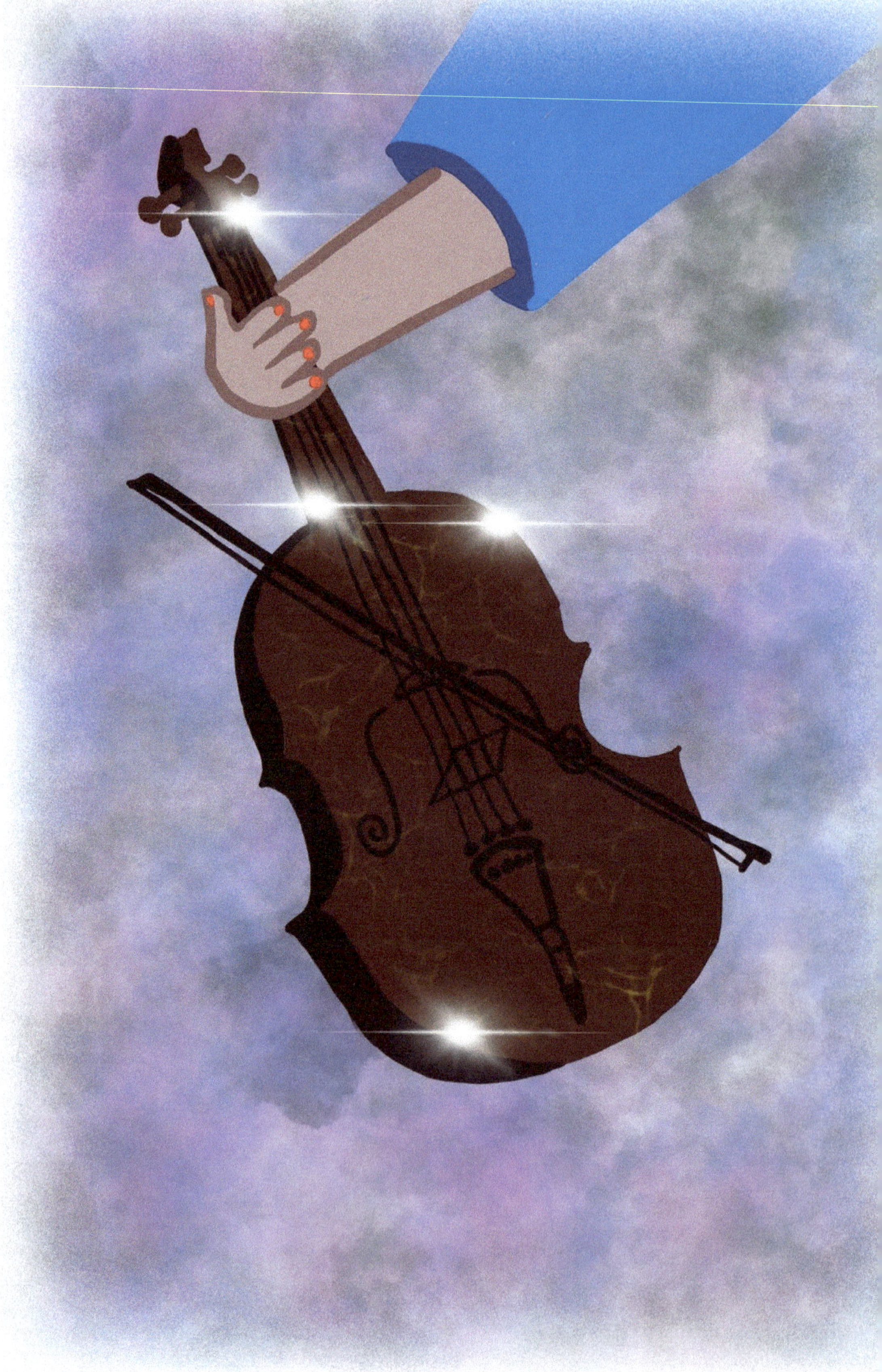

As Mayuri held the new violin, both Sensei and Mayuri were struck with **Isshin Denshin** (what the mind thinks instantly the heart transmits). They both saw simultaneously that the violin and the lacquer box had the same glossy sheen. The two objects not only looked alike but even smelt and felt similar. The violin had the same nostalgic fragrance which was emitted from the lacquer box and both gave the same smooth feeling when her hands gently caressed them. Mayuri perceived a deep connection between both her new violin and the glistening wooden artwork. This brought immense **Yorokobi** (inner happiness) to Mayuri and inspired her to request Kadota Sensei to teach her the vibrato again. Sensei was deeply touched that Mayuri had finally found her calling in life – **Ikigai** (goal, meaning and purpose in life). A very deep sense of contentment emerged simultaneously within the minds and hearts of both Sensei and Mayuri. Unspoken understanding had established in their **Kokoro** (hearts).

Trying hard to hold back her tears, Kadota Sensei nodded gently when Mayuri said, "Will you now teach me the vibrato?"

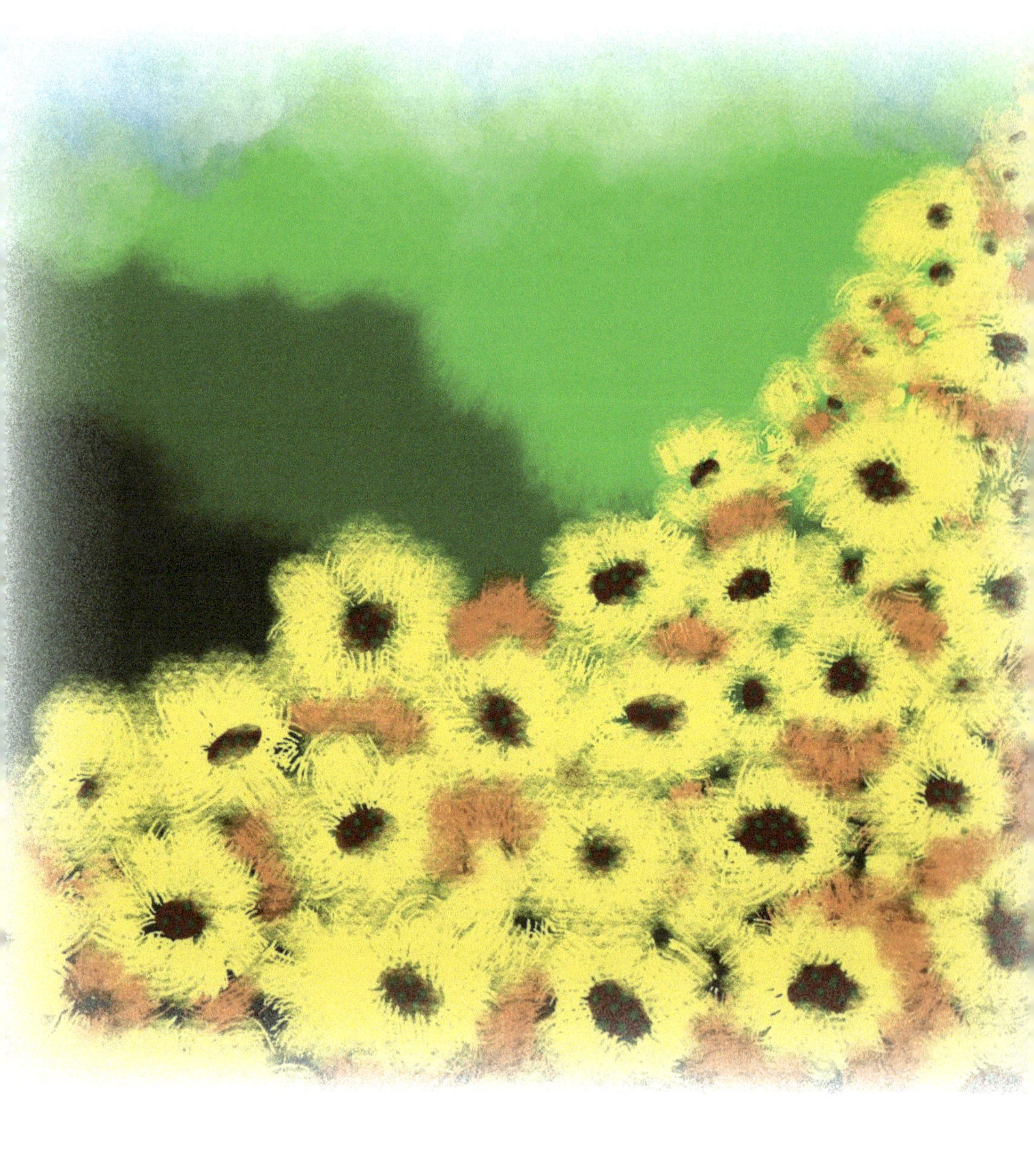

With great devotion Mayuri played Bach's Minuet in G major and there was passion in her vibrato like never seen or heard before. Thereafter, the violin became an important and integral part of Mayuri's daily life.

Mayuri practiced her violin relentlessly for hours each day while standing and looking directly out of her window. The window faced a field abundant with wild orange and yellow sunflowers.

It was the field upon which Matsumoto Mayuri's home once stood.

There was no looking back now. Mayuri's flame of passion had ignited, and she was being nurtured everyday by Kadota Sensei to become the professional violinist she is today. Along with Sensei, Mayuri's enchanting lotus lacquer box – her good old friend – had given her the strength and spirit to achieve her professional goals. She was now performing concerts all over Japan.

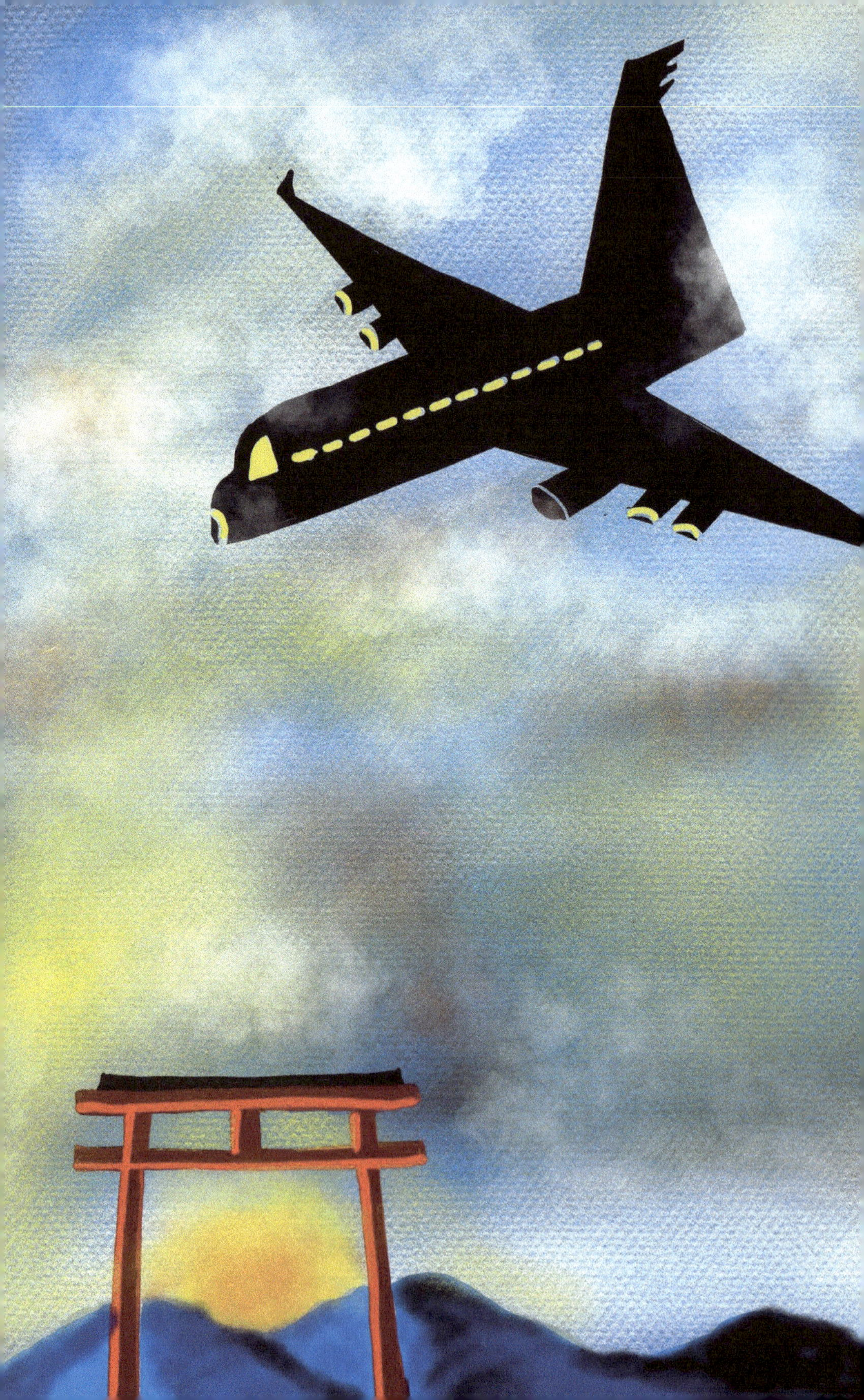

On her successful trip to Moscow, she had returned with a new best friend – the violin shaped sunflower lacquer box which was carefully placed inside the lapis lazuli stoneware for extra protection! The sunflower box will now provide Mayuri with added support in enhancing her talent and always looking at the bright side of life.

With her two precious friends, Mayuri considered herself to be doubly fortunate. One taught her to rise above all the trials and tribulations in life and the other taught her to bring in sunshine no matter how gloomy the situation may look. Her life, like the lacquer boxes, was made up of layers and layers of hard work, pain and resilience. She was now the polished, refined, and talented violinist, Mayuri Matsumoto, who had risen above the pain and hardships encountered from the Great Hanshin Earthquake of January 17, 1995. Over the years, Mayuri blossomed like the lotus and sunflower on her lacquer boxes. Kadota Sensei, who meant the world to Mayuri, was like the deep blue earth coloured Lapis Lazuli, who protected Mayuri and assisted her in reaching where she is today.

As the plane descended smoothly towards the runway of Osaka's Kansai International Airport, her mind had excitedly raced over to Sensei. She could not wait to share with Sensei all the details of her magical, sensational and shining performance. She also could not wait to show and tell Sensei all about her new magnificent gift!

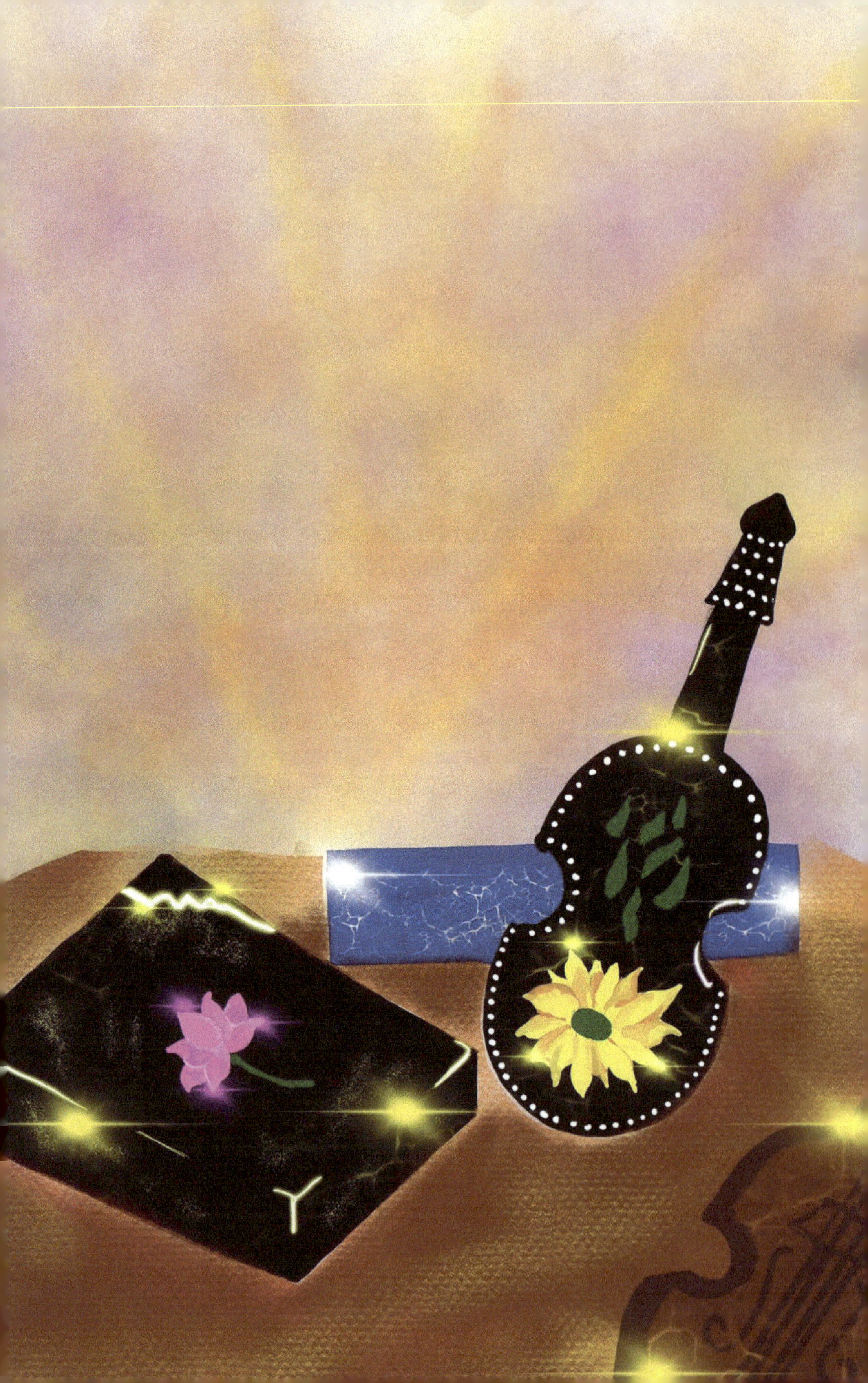

Mayuri had already decided on how she would keep both her old and new best friends close to each other in her bedroom.

The Japanese lotus lacquer box and the Russian sunflower lacquer box were going to be placed next to the Afghani lapis lazuli box along with Sensei's precious gift – her greatest friend with whom she will always travel – her new radiant Stradivarius violin. They would all continue to inspire and motivate Mayuri to keep her passion ever glowing and shining.

Feeling on top of the world, though the plane had already landed, Mayuri's thoughts had taken flight and she was imagining how immaculately she would perform at her upcoming concert with the Tokyo Metropolitan Symphony Orchestra. She will present her masterpiece vibrato during Mozart's Violin Concerto No 5. She will touch the heart strings of her audience just as her baton would touch the strings of her violin, making Sensei's and Mayuri's dream come true. With synchronicity they both believed **Hibi Kore Kou Jitsu** (everyday is a good day by focusing on the present).

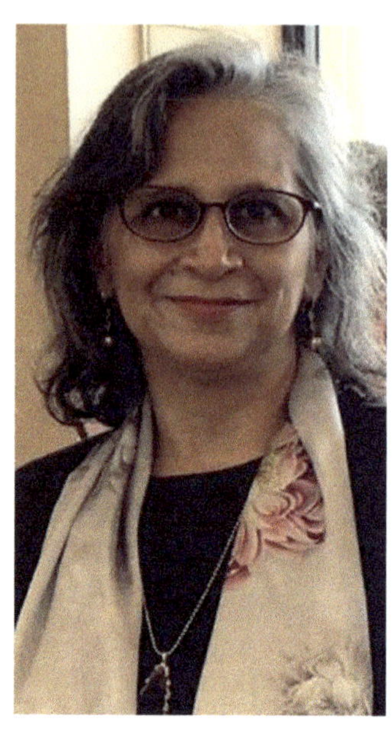

About the Author

Parul, a Singapore citizen, has a multicultural upbringing – born in India, grew up in Japan, studied in the US and lived for short periods of time in Afghanistan, Russia and the UK. While raising her children in Kobe and Singapore, she enjoyed reading to them a variety of Japanese, Indian and Western children's books which ignited her dream to write a new genre of an illustrated storybook for all ages. The impact of the Great Hanshin Earthquake in her hometown Kobe further stirred Parul to write a healing story using her own collection of lacquerware and cross-cultural artifacts/boxes. Through this story, she hopes that children will be inspired to find their passion, purpose and path in life – **Ikigai**.

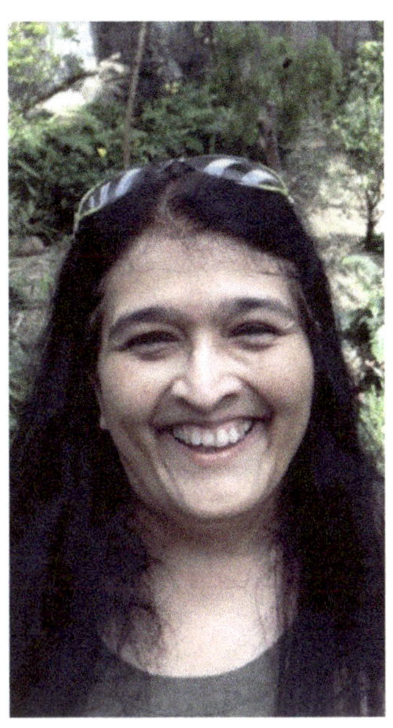

About the Illustrator

Radhika Iyer is an artist who lives in Singapore. A student of art she has had a few solo exhibitions of her pen and ink works and has also held shows of upcoming artists from India over the years. She has done varied art related projects working with different materials. Recently she had an exhibition of her work with clay, the proceeds of which were donated to a children's NGO in India. She is constantly experimenting with various techniques and textures and enjoys the process. Art for her is continuous learning experience.

Acknowledgements

Gratitude to my family and friends in Kobe and Singapore for awakening me to write this story which was nestled away for many years.

Lightning Source UK Ltd.
Milton Keynes UK
UKHW051937201022
410842UK00015B/82